January 2

To: Teresa

love lift

with appreciation,

Gregory John Saxby

Sipping Tea

Gregory John Saxby

Suite 300 - 990 Fort St
Victoria, BC, V8V 3K2
Canada

www.friesenpress.com

First Edition — 2017

My thanks to so many who have encouraged this work with kind words and warm affection. Special thanks to Jessica Moore. Attending her performance at Lake Superior State University inspired me to move forward with this work.

Cover photo by Gerry Sproule, a friend.

ISBN
978-1-5255-1458-6 (Hardcover)
978-1-5255-1459-3 (Paperback)
978-1-5255-1460-9 (eBook)

1. POETRY, CANADIAN

Distributed to the trade by The Ingram Book Company

Sipping Tea

I picture her
sipping tea
in elegant profile:

Saucer in her left hand,
cup raised to her lips.
gazing through the panes
of twenty-six dimensions[1].

Gazing at the seas,
the seas
that hold all time and tears,
sorrows and fears,
buried at infinite depths.

I feel her waiting,
waiting
for the sight of me,
as I do for her,

Keeping watch.
keeping watch for
the perfect reproduction
of our best intentions.

1 Certain equations in "String Theory" predict the existence of up to twenty-six dimensions.

Contents

Refuge

Remember

Rappin'

Reflection

Acceptance

Names

When I met her she was Dena.
Over many years she was also
Diana, Diana Lee, and Diane.
Her full given name was Dena Diana Lee Mary Dolores.

We had forty wonder-filled years together.
On April 2nd, 2015
a large tumour was found in her right lung.
She died on August 16th of that year—
two days short of her fifty-eighth birthday.

I can't remember one harsh word,
let alone an argument between us.

She needed all those names to hold the love she had to give.
I never worried if I would see heaven when I died.
I was already there.

Dena Diana Lee Mary Dolores left it to me
to remember
and to celebrate
our love.

I Don't Know (Memoriam)

I don't know why
I open my eyes;
I will never see
the like of her.

The music of my life,
its rhythm and meaning,
her sunlight gleaming:
my food, my fodder,
pushing up love
from its roots
in my soul.

You see the world, now,
through my eyes;
you breathe
my breaths.

You are the beat
of my heart.

I will cry the oceans dry
for you, my love.
You are my life,
my love forever—

I wait for the day
We reunite
in God's eternal light.

About Poems

A Poem Should

A poem should
be heartfelt—
heaven sent—
stir passion,
be powerful,
awaken dreams and
imagination,
have lines of beauty and awe—
tickle a fancy or two—
find a bell to ring true,
have rhythm and rhyme,
enchant the reader,
transport time.

Take A Poem Home

Take a poem home tonight
let it linger till dawn.

Find it a soft robe to put on,
let it curl up
beside your warm fire
on the rug of your soul.

It could spark
a dream or two—
perhaps a reverie
to see you through
life's wistful times.

Add it to your repertoire,
keep it in a cozy drawer
there ready to spring to life
when you encounter tumult and strife.

It may slake a thirst
or sate a hunger,
lighten a mood,
fill you with spiritual food
and nourish better days.

Give your soul reason to praise
this life.

Our Introduction

Our Introduction

I joked that my jaw still ached
from the way it dropped when
I first saw Dena. Not a joke.
A straight true fact.

I was arranging my float at the
till. It was a sunny, bright day—
a Tuesday or Wednesday in early
June—as I started my shift at The
Beer Store.

The door buzzer sounded.
I looked up.
There she was.
A glowing radiance to rival
that summer sun.

I can remember back at light speed,
through forty years of yesterdays,
to that moment.

"Oh! Wow!" I thought.
I had seen movies with
Brigitte Bardot, Sophia Loren,
Jayne Mansfield and Marilyn Monroe,
but I had never been
in the presence of such beauty.

Beauty can betray years, so I
challenged her
to present proof of age
to purchase the beer she wanted.

"I don't have any.
I left my purse at home.
We're moving."

"I'm sorry, miss. I can't serve you."

She left unhappy. Very unhappy,
as I was later told.

Saturday night of that same week,
a buddy and I walked into the bar
of the Algonquin Hotel in Sault Ste. Marie.
Who was sitting at a table
loaded with drinks?

Uh-huh. She saw me.
Up off her chair like a rocket,
she came up to me—
"Don't you tell anyone!"

I didn't. It wasn't my business to do so.
That is how we came to be.

Had I not refused to sell her that beer,
she likely would not have noticed me.
I don't think men said no to her
very often.

From then on, neither did I.

Inspiration

The blinding inspiration of her love
I will never live apart from.

It is in my heart forever.

It was
  a serendipitous conjunction of circumstance.

Now I live in
  a shell-shocked daze in
  the absence of her loving presence.

To be whole again,
I must await the inevitable—
The conjunction of our forevers.

She will always be
  that young girl
    who led me
      to a dream life
        I could never imagine
          to be mine.

Her dancing rhymes—
her rhythms and times
of joy and laughter:

Percolating wonders of a wild flower
who shared with me
her happily ever after.

I Don't Know

I don't know why
I open my eyes;
I will never see
the like of her.

The music of my life,
its rhythm and meaning,
her sunlight gleaming:
my food, my fodder
pushing up love
from its roots
in my soul.

You see the world, now,
through my eyes:
you breathe
my breaths.

You are the beat
of my heart.

Love is become
a cruel country;
a bland epilogue
of mournful mornings.

The loose threads
of my sorrow
litter the floor.

This is love's
false economy of happiness . . .
isolated showers of hope
mine my soul
for nuggets of peace.

Word Search is empty,
joy/sorrow un-reconciled.

Washing up, thrashing about . . .
nuggets of peace....
just laying there.

Letters to Diana

That Night

You had been fighting
for your life for weeks—
exhaustion building,
breathing shallow,
a twitch of your eyes
here and there.

This the sum of your
once vigorous, loving self.
Were you now in life's replay?
Your courageous spirit
no longer able to will
the body forward.

Your determination to stay
and love me forever,
soon to be delivered
to the ephemeral,

unable to speak
even the softest of goodbyes;
unable to purse your lips
for one last sweet kiss.

You refuse to say goodbye?

So do I.

In The Evening

In the evening
I fall on our bed,
exhausted.

Exhausted by the loss of you.

Yet, hopeful.

Hopeful that sleep will come,
that dreams will come,
that you will come—
come to reassure me—
reassure me of your safety.

That you have well-being.

That you have any being
at all.

That you would come to me
restored.

Restored to your natural
vitality and joy,
your loving nature
un-impinged.

Do you not know how to find me?

I know you are trying,
as I try to find you.

To speak to you,
to caress you,
to hold you in my arms
(your beauty and your love
transporting me
to other-worldly delight).

Other worldly.

Yes.

That is what has become of you,
of me,
of us.

Façade Of Shadows

This life I have now
this façade of shadows

your light just a memory

warm, yes
wonderful, yes
thankful, yes
but just a shadow
of what was.

It is what it is
and that is: Past.

You have passed
from this life
from my life
now a netherworld's
sweet spirit.

I struggle to find you
I search and search and search

through my weeping

through my yearning for what was
but can never be again;
we exist apart, my love,
joined only in spirit and memory.

Quixotic signals you send
but these do not mend me;
only perplex and confuse.

I awoke this morning
and for a moment
found some satisfying energy—

then it crashed
in a wave of tears.

Every instant I realize
you are truly not here.
You will not reappear,
it breaks me down.

I will not answer
the ring of the phone
to hear your sweet voice:
"I'm heading home!
See you in thirty minutes!
Put the coffee on!"

This house of ours
is your hallowed ground:
it holds all our years of joy.

But it is cold comfort
without the warmth
of your sweetest voice,
your loving attention.

You wring tears from me
like a wet towel wrung—

weeping: tears for your beauty
weeping: tears for your voice
weeping: tears for your warmth

weeping: I weep for your happy nature
weeping: I weep for your innocent love

My God, Bijou! How I mourn you!
It shakes and shreds my very being!

I would sell my soul for one word
heard in your loving voice!

I still stand on my feet
like Rocky Balboa
barely conscious of anything
save my sorrow for you—

for you: the best part of me
for you: my truest consolation
for you: my whole joy in life.

"Blessed Are Those Who Mourn, For They Shall Be Comforted"

ONE MORE TIME

Dawn, and another day without you.
It crushes my spirit.
It empties my heart.

Once so full, so vibrant
now dead and dull.
Just a few grains,
a few threads of thin,
hollow hope remain.

This strange, scary world:
life without
your loving presence.

The bleak panorama of your death;
the haunting void of your absence.

A facsimile of normal sprouts—
then erupts in an ocean of tears.

Soul-splitting oblivion.
This hopeless, hopeless despair
of life without you:
the most vital of all my organs.

What I would not give
to hear your voice.
Its tenderness and care.
Its laughter and joy.

One more time.
One more time.
Just one more time.

Take my soul—
take all my forever,
my Forever Girl,
my Starburst Girl.

Just give me
one more time.

Whence Have You Gone?

Soul mate, whence have you gone?

Into the air?
Into the wind?

To some mystical dimension
of infinite continuums?

To the Promised Land of Glories
to behold?

Are you a whisper
of shared memory?

Are you hidden; a thin frequency
of vibrating energy strings?

Are you with the Saviour
in resurrected glory?

Do you await
my arrival?

I know you long for me
as I mourn your absence
—*are* you absent?

No, No, No.

You are still living
where you always
have been—

DEEP IN MY SOUL.

I Mourn You

I mourn you
in a make-believe half-life
of shadows and shallows;

I plow hollow furrows of sorrow,
searching for the warmth
of your sun.

What terrifies me is:
this trek has just begun.

What hurts most
amongst horror's hosts is:
the loss of my centre of being,
passed into the unseen.

Warm memories are not
the same as the vibrant life
you gave me.
I cannot replace
the blinding inspiration
of you, Bijou.

I stare at that stark reality:
the headstone,
your lifetime carved there
from year of being
to year of passing.

I resolve to proclaim your wonder,
to give those cold numbers
meaning.

Love is the only word
I can think of.

For Lovers

Valentine's Day

Valentine's Day
I lit a candle for her.
No—for us.

This day to celebrate love
so precious/fragile/enduring . . .

That forever of emotion
once felt and never forgotten.

Seldom recaptured.

I warn you: tread lightly its path.

Dance Of Life

She told me
She loved me
with every waking glance
She told me
She loved me
as through our life
we danced—

a dance so joyous
it could not help
but be
her song of life
through all eternity—

this joyous song
She left to me
that I might know
Her happy glee

Her glee for all things found
Her glee for glory bound
bound to my soul and heart—
never by death
set apart—

She tells me
She loves me
with every
waking glance
She tells me
She loves me
as through our lives
we dance

Walk Me

Walk me through midnight—
wear starlight on your sleeve!

You could light a city.

Weave the tapestry
of breathless whispers,
silk-smooth night in your eyes!

They could hold the oceans.

Still, still, still
vesper mists—
kissing my cheek
like a Chopin nocturne.

Timeless in space.

Morning

In the morning haze
of lovers' exultations,
entwined as one,
the day's begun.

Anticipations unknown:
the softness , the warmth
the tenderness;
this morning dew of passion
the liquorice of love!

Peace for companion souls abounds.

Elixir; intoxication;
spirit sounds of life
shared as one:
one heart, one soul, one love,

one kiss.

Each Day

each day to be born again
each day to remember when

first we met
first we kissed
first we embraced

to become this:

this love
this life
this thing sublime

the beauty of which
is ours through time

each day born again

Here And Now

We stand
in the here and now:
reciting our promise and vow;
stretching to reach—
our lips to beseech.

We share
our first kiss:
as our love we enlist;
for eternity sublime—
frozen in a crystal of time.

Love Blossoms

Love blossoms in profusion:
welcome;
no intrusion.

Fragile cups of hope
quench a thirst,
for what?

Infinity?
Humanity?
Meaning?

Did I meet you,
dreaming,
some soul-swept night?

Did we embrace,
couple in our spirituality?

Such questions
from fragile blossoms—
blown away
in the next gust of life.

Expressions

You're full of expressions
that taunt me and tease,
you conquer my sleep
with sweet memory.

You know that to love me
there's nothing to please
except call me to love you
with such wistful ease.

Like strings on a puppet
your touch masters me,
like the spell of a sorceress
that bends me to knee.

I will be waiting
till broken and dead
for the gypsies of fortune
we never had.

Addiction

My beautiful addiction:
I crave
her full, soft lips—
sensuous, moist, and warm—
surrounding me,
drawing me in.

Eyes glowing with adoring sparkle;
a waterfall of soft words
in a honey-sweet voice.

Sweet, soft touch,
I rest on her
ample bosom:
my comforting oasis.

The void of
the Death

is filling . . .

with new air,
new hope,
new light
burrowing through night,
escaping the sad furrows
of the killing fields.

I am her addict
she, my delicious drug.

I cannot see over
the lights shining on me.

is this the centre-
stage of love?

Heart stopped
Heart stopping beauty
Heartbreak passion?

An embrace I
love too much.

I am a void
without her.

So many echoes
of the delight
of my life—
Only ever once,
I thought,
and yet—
Here I am again.

With my sole comfort.
With my soul salvation.

A reflection
near perfection ,
I sit in perplexed

disbelief.

Whispers

Whispers of love
invade my home
when I am safe
in bed.

Sisters of Rome comfort
my thoughts
when I am lying, feeling
dead.

But ask them
to explain
my hopes of love;
their faces
turn quite red.

With wisdom my wealth
I ask them
to take donations
of bread.

But fish is their life
and to Jesus a wife,
they've forgotten
what He said.

Peter's ghost
unfolds his chair
and sits inside
my head.

He was there
when the fishers came
and found their words
for the dead.

And as the dawn
sleeps in my room
I take an
empty chair.

I write on mirrors
and drink the tears
your lips left
in my hair.

My eyes close
much too soon
and I see them
everywhere:

The Sisters and men,
the fishers and dead,
and the whispers
that once were there.

I Must Confess

I must confess
the wisdom of your body;
confess enjoying
your rapacious appetite
and wanton absolution.

My young lion,
you claw too wildly,
your cries of pride
betray your lair;
the scissors that cut your hair
as a cub.

My friend,
he seeks only
to tame you.

I hope to name you.

All The Sweet Girls

all the sweet girls
all the sweet girls
they be home soon
they be home

they be gathering
they be gathering
at forever's doorstep

with love in their touch
and happy ever after
in their eyes

honey in their voices
music on their breath

they be waiting
they be waiting
their arms wide open

they be ready
they be ready
to look every hell
ever invented
in the face

they be ready
they be ready
to wave them away
leaving no trace

just with a flick
of their pretty wrists

wave away pain
wave away sorrow
wave away every
broken tomorrow

wave away sadness
wave away grief
send away, send away
send away deep

all the sweet girls
they be singing
love them now
you know
what they're bringing

they be waiting
they be waiting true
remember this
when you fret
what to do

kiss the sweet girls
with their rosy red cheeks
they carry peace
they know what you seek

soon you be joining their bliss
soon you be given that kiss

that kiss
you know you lack,

lack so deep
you cannot sleep

love all the sweet girls
love them true
they be waiting
waiting for you

all the sweet girls
all the sweet girls
they know you so well
they can rescue
and keep you
keep you from hell

my sweet girl
takes the pain away

take all the pain away
all the pain away

come, sweet girl
come take me
fill me to the top

fill my lovin' cup
fill it up
fill me up

again and

again and

again

We Were Lovers

We were lovers
long before we met.
Our spirits co-mingled
in eternity's ether.

The children of
cosmic intent.

A rampant intoxication.

How else to explain
the water without rain,
the light without sun,
the growth without soil.

The simple ease of it,
without complication;
placing the other
before self.

A seamless union.

Now: we cry soft, gentle tears
soaking the soil
with longing murmurs.

Now: we warm ourselves
with memorial radiance.

Now: we confront yawning chasms
of separation.

Now: we ferret all the dimensions
for some kind of path
to reunion.

Refuge

Ref-uge (ref`yuj)n.

1. shelter or protection from danger , trouble, etc.; safety;security.
2. any person , thing ,or action providing or seeming to provide safety , security , or comfort.

Silos of Solitude

Silos of solitude
surround my grief.

Anxious sentinels,
they turn to gaze at
the heavens—
lest any rays of hope
my sorrow may leaven.

Attempt escape?

Forty years of growing
together as one?
How can I escape my*self*?

For she is me as
I am she.

With allies shall I confer?
to organize a cabal,
a breakout, a flight?

Amass a league of
emotional refugees,
each evicted
from their Eden of Love:
A fellowship of the afflicted.

Perhaps a pardon.
—A medical exemption
For the sake of mercy.

We will rally our spirits
We will rally our souls
We will rally our love
for compassionate roles.

We will gather at the arch,
We will travel through our grief.
We will march over the arch.

The Arch

A bridge
—over pain
—over loss

A bridge
to vistas
where the
bright light
of eternal love
and peace
beckons
—beckons to the
eye of the soul
—oh to know the
peace and rest
that only
the eternal
can give!

—That heals all wounds
—That restores all being

Being in the
here and now
—no past
—no future
—nothing more

to be clutched
or desperately
grasped at
—only the now
and the here
so filled with love.........

There is no more
to be said
—To quiet
the most
profound lament
—To lighten
the deepest
melancholy
—To illuminate
the darkest heart
—To reconcile
the most rueful
regret.

shedding
the cocoons
of sorrow
and grief
taking flight

—unburdened
—transformed
floating in the
always
and
forever

Like butterflies.

Written to commemorate
ARCH hospice Butterfly Release Ceremony.

Comfort Food

With the passion of
your art
to fashion meals
set apart
from the ordinary;

the tender care
of that special fare
to bless those passing;

surrendering to their needs
to find the food
that feeds
their bodies and spirits;

to reassure and console
that when the body fails
the soul
will still thrive—
with picture-perfect presentation.

Dedicated to Erik Nowack, Chef Extraordinaire,
ARCH Hospice

You Say

You say write a poem
for me to read.
You say we gather here
because we need
so much more
than we find alone.

You say write a poem.
We can make of it
a home.

A home to find comfort
A home to gain solace
A home where angels
make light the load
we must carry in our grief.

You say write a poem
to celebrate the Spirit:
This life of creation.

"Write a poem—
find your home,
find your way!"

You say
write a poem.

I need it.

I will feed it
to those others with
thirst and hunger.

You say write a poem.

I don't want
to be alone.

Dedicated to Tiffany Caicco, counsellor,
ARCH Hospice

Remember

re•mem•ber
/rəˈmembər/
verb

1. to have in or bring to your mind someone or something from your past;
2. to keep something necessary in mind;
3. to bear someone in mind by making them a gift or by mentioning them in prayer;
4. (to remember someone to) to pass on greetings from one person to another

o.e.d. 4th edition

Memory

The memory I want
is of you:

Your sparkling eyes
I remember
Your laughing voice
I remember
Your loving touch,
I remember

While I remember,
I am loving you.
The memory I want
is of that bright summer's day
that was the years of our love.

Your exciting wonder
I remember
Your adventurous spirit
I remember
Your tender care
I remember

My only sustenance
is my memory of loving you.
My memory of you,
my eternal love.

Your faithful help
I remember
Your love of nature
I remember
Your happy voice joy
I remember

Bijou—
I will never change
I will never falter
I will never doubt.

I will live with you,
in memory,
in our house.

This house
that you made—
made so loving
made so peaceful.

My harbour from worry
My harbour from strife
My resting place and yours.

Our perfect peace together.

You fade into memory—
but your memory
does not fade.

Summer Day

That summer day
that bright, bright day
and your playful poses . . .

I think of you.

I wash my face
with my tears.

Such a beauty
chose me.
Such a loving spirit
wanted me.

There were more miracles in you
than in any Testament.

Now I live
in the what was
and the what will be,
without you in
the here and now.

In the air
In the wind
Where our next chapter
will begin.

This girl
with a love for me—
the most perfect
a man could ever know—
my forever love.

This girl, for love's
least accomplished
foot soldier.

I Enlist

I enlist,
lost love's wounded
foot soldier.

I stand ready
in my tattered uniform;
epaulettes in order
medals and ribbons
of your bravery
proudly pinned to my chest.

At the ready,
I salute your command
to attention.

Soon the trumpets will sound
their call to action.

A noble cause awaits!
To retrieve my hope—
To rescue my reasoning—
To revive my breathing.

I listen and listen for
the sound of your voice,
the commencement of our
campaign for everlasting unity.

This is the tragedy beyond
my comprehension,
this cruellest irony:
my abiding joy
is now my grievous sorrow.

Diana gave me a watch on our first anniversary. I wore it every day for forty years. Aside from two or three new batteries, it kept perfect time. In the years after her death, I have had to send it for repair twice.

The Watch

Since her death
the watch is troubled;
engraved as her token,
it is broken.

Old temptations rage,
I fall too easy:
Pain my crutch—
my rationale for
the fires of Hell.

I try to patch over
my heart hole;
it sucks me down,
where there is
no air
no fair
no peace
no quiet.

There is lunging
and lurching:
no more churching.
Empty promises
I hear,
uttered to deaf ears.

The hours, the days
go wandering off,
wandering off,
and the watch
is troubled;
its hands are frozen.

Everything beautiful
reminds me of you.
But the warmth, the sparkle,
Is fading,
fading
into memory.

The memory of the
beautiful girl
who wanted

me.

Humour

I'm not sure
but I heard a rumour:
Saxby could write
with humour.

Some said they'd
pay real money
to see or hear
something funny.

Would he prance and preen
like a joker;
would he change
that face
that belongs to poker?

In The Parking Lot

In the parking lot
of the supermarket
a bright, sunny,
December day.

So rare, I thought:
a blest gift from
my departed love.

Struggling with my wounds
I loaded my groceries
from the shopping cart
into the car.

Turning, I caught sight of her—
such a vision!
Tall and slender,
so well dressed:
an appealing wonder.

A wide, sunny smile,
just like the day and
and the sun itself: so radiant—

and looking, looking
directly at me!
At me?
Do I know you?
Should I remember you?
Surely I have not forgotten.

Are you God's Angel then,
sent to comfort my sorrow?
Could this be some new beginning?

But so soon after
My loss?
Could there be such a wonder?

She drew closer, still radiant
with her warm, inviting smile.
Softly, in honey-sweet tones, she spoke:
"Are you through with that cart?
I could use it."

The Trouble With Sleeping Late

The trouble with sleeping late
is:
you're late.
Meds schedule's broken,
You're in a rush
to be ready—
even if it's ready
for nothing.

Behind, behind
on all those important things.

Face it:
you're out of sync
you feel you're
on the brink
of some lurking disaster.

Something that requires
time to master—
time you haven't got
because you forgot
to set the clock.

Now you're running late—
in a quandary—
no time to vacuum,
no time for laundry.

Late for lunch,
feeling the crunch,
the bed unmade,
hair un-kempt
the doorway un-swept.

I'm the Mad Hatter.

I've no time to relax
no time to face the fact:
it's trouble
when sleeping late.

No time to set the fire
I'm swallowed in my mire.

I finish the day
exhausted by the race—
tomorrow is too hard to face . . .

I'll likely sleep late.

Stratford 1952

The Depression . . . over
"Hey buddy , can you spare—"

The War . . . over
"Today, Canada declared a—"

The country takes a deep breath
like a drowning man's
first gasp of air
in minutes.

Deep, deep, deep—
fill your lungs . . .
feel the ecstasy of relief.

Years of telegrams "We regret to inform you—"
Years of phone calls "Is this the *** residence?"
Years of approaches "I'm sorry to tell you—"

"He was so . . ."
"He'll be missed so . . ."
"How are you all . . .
"Is everything . . ."

Now over. Now done.

Breathe in again . . . exhale!

Sleeping so long to even before memory
Optimism is now stirring.

The air is bedewed with hope.

Time to dream again . . .
the sound of seeds
springing to life from
the bedrock brotherhood
of the people,
their solid, flinty resolution
tempered and forged
in the fire of those
twin Hells of Depression and War.

A suffocating lid
Is finally pried off;
Hope no longer rationed
by years of scraping by.

All this, in my beginning
I remember . . .

It was:
  milk delivered to the door
  by a horse-drawn cart;

It was:
    milk in glass bottles,
    bulbs at the neck
    for the butter fat;

It was:
    iceboxes full of
    block ice, delivered by cart and
    straw everywhere;

It was:
    the backyard rhubarb patch
    with no arguments
    just sweet-tasting pie;

It was:
    the downtown dairy bar—
    milk, shakes, ice cream—
    "A vanilla shake please,"
    "Ten cents."

It was:
    Sunday Church services—
    a full house, all
    thanking God for deliverance;

It was:

watching steam locomotives
clanking, puffing jets of vapour
at the yard—
chunks of coal strewn
by the rails;

It was:

coal bins and ash shakers
in basement furnaces
growling with each shovelful—
coal dust rising
with each delivery
that fell like Niagara down the chute;

It was:

the O'Cedar factory
at the corner
one house down—
clean sweepers,
unused rail siding,
weeded and overgrown;

It was:

men in peaked caps
riding bicycles to work with
pantleg clips,
pipes clenched in teeth—

Content to have work?
Relieved to have survived?
Saved, by chance, to have a future?

It was:
Stratford-upon-Avon;

It was:
schools named
Romeo and Juliet
the talismans of future love;

It was:
the time before
a family car—
walks back home
riding my father's sure shoulders;

It was:
the freedom of the first
two-wheeler—
that exhilarating balance and speed!

It was:
pipe tobacco in humidors
pocket pouches and
tweed jackets with
leather elbow patches;

It was:
  wooden barrels with metal bindings
  to catch rainwater
  at the eaves and
  enamel ware, often chipped
  (plastic unheard of);

It was:
  heavy, whirring appliances—
  wringer washers and
  clothes lines everywhere;

It was:
  Lionel train sets
  Matchbox Cars and Dinky Toys;
  Mock battles in the gravel floor
  Of the old garage;

It was:
  Gielgud at The Festival
  addressing schoolchildren—
  that great man making time
  as all great men do
  to tend the garden
  of our future;

The future, a precious notion;
The future, our reason for motion;

That next breath—
The next shard of hope—
salvaged from broken dreams!

This was the beginning
of everything precious.

As I recall it, I had seen an ad in the local newspaper inviting applicants to interview for positions for ad copy and/or greeting cards. I had written some poems at college, but dismissed the idea of this interview as irrelevant to what I wrote.

Diana did not. Without my knowing, she arranged for me to interview with a very "gracious man".

Gracious Man

He was a gracious man:
greying hair,
well-groomed,
well-dressed:
jacket and tie
tasteful.

Refined manners,
excellent diction , phrasing;
words well-chosen,
(a degree in literature,
no doubt).

Perhaps his family were
patrons of the arts
but hard times have befallen.

He is older now,
And looking to reclaim . . .
something.

This excursion
to find an artistic
and commercial truce
between
the warring factions of persona.

He is more than a greeting card,
He is more than bland sympathies;
more than this
succession of hotel rooms
in cities and towns
of low standing.

His civility is untarnished
but his spirit is straining
at the leashes of necessity.

For twenty minutes—
to renew the early promise
with a young man
in whom he saw himself,
                                        perhaps—
he read the work
(with interest);
made a mild suggestion.

He predicted a future
he considered inevitable:
"You'll wind up a VP
of something, somewhere,
there's no doubt."

I wound up
the happiest man in the world.

Rappin'

In February 2016, poet Jessica Care Moore
gave a reading at Lake Superior State University,
Sault Sainte Marie , Michigan.

She said that when she was living in New York
City, she was given the nickname " Jesse James"
by friends.

Jessica

Jesse James:
loaded gun
primed for passion

for her art:
for her living love
a breathtaking soul

hated to leave:
one evening
was more than
I could touch

broke out:
in passion spots
all over my soul,
my "chi" gone
critical

I'll be awhile:
reading this book*[2]
drinking in
the passion
and sage

....

2 *Sunlight through Bullet Holes* by Jessica Moore.

(barely able to
turn the page)

I bookmark:
with tissue
to catch my tears

pure intoxication:
every line I read
I say *Wow!*
a wow like
my paradise beginning

Jesse James:
sun and rain
wind and fire
all the elements
loaded and primed

You Think

You think you got rhythm
You think you got beat
You think you can shake me
like dust from your feet

You think you got swagger
You think you got game
You think you can 'dis me
and call down my name

You think you got order
You think you got rule
You think you can dupe me
and play me for fool

You think you got muscle
You think you got style
You think you can blind me
with smoke and with guile

You think you got Heaven
You think you got life—

All you bring to me
is sadness and strife.

When It All Comes Down

This is when
it all comes down,
with smoke and mirrors
for President—

When it all comes down
to shameless charlatans of the night,
their shallow legends
of empty deceit—

When it all comes down,
When it all comes down—

When angels rip off
their haloes
When sorrow comes
like thunder
(rolling across a thousand years,
ready to inflict pain
in the name of purity)—

When it all comes down
the drums and whistles
of deadly days,
wrecking balls stalking
and dead men walking—

When it all comes down, brothers,
When it all comes down, sisters,

When your world ends
what will your spirit
send back to us?

A deeper meaning?

Will these be the eyes
of eternity?

Staring down,
staring down
forever's river—
staring down to its sea—

When it all comes down
you'd better find
your hallowed ground,
you'd better stake
your claim,
you'd better know
your name—

That name that makes
you unique,
that name that
God will seek—

Do you hear that thunder?

Used By Permission

I never gave them permission
to oppress in my name—
to harass, to ridicule, to demean—
but I did not speak out,
I did not shout it out
for all to hear, to see:
"You do not have permission
to inflict such misery!"

With each insulting,
stupid story
or joke,
I did not speak out—
I did not turn away.

So they assumed my permission
and that is my shame.

I let them use my name.

I gave permission by omission.

Ain't Gonna Be

Ain't gonna be today.
No birdsongs in your fire spray,
no prayin' on bended knee.

Will I be the feather
in your cap
when you awake
from your nap?

No barkers at the mic,
no flyers by the kite

Lookin' to catch
lightnin' in a bottle;
lookin' to give life
full throttle.

Ain't gonna be today.
You gonna beseech
the icons you preach?

You gonna fall down
the gilded gown,
the rabbit hole of love?

You gonna blow holes
through time 'n space,
hold'n memories in hand and face?

For what
To fill your gut?
To feed your soul?
To dig under ground
like a feckless mole?

You just gotta know what's there
You just gotta know what's there
You just gotta know what's there

You got a feather in your cap yet?

Trapped

Trapped between a rock
and a hard place:
rock-hard granite,
gravel, coarse,
his voice , broken.

Lost in an ocean of questions,
surfing tsunamis of
good intentions.

"Don't lose that board!"
"Don't loose your grip!"

Strip-search your soul.

Impeach your reverential icons,
eternity is watching, waiting.

Border wars, intrusions,
incursions ravaging
the pastures of reason,
the perpetual gunfire
of dreams broken.

Crashing like blood-soaked boarders
on the breakers of
sumptuous arrogance.

Sorrow their thunder.

Turn Hollow

Do your dreams turn hollow
on the twisted road
you follow?

Do your excuses burn
like a solar flare?

Do you reach for peace
and find the cupboard bare?

Do your ears ring
as bullets sing
the litany of the fallen?

Heroes turned broken,
muzzle flashes are
the only words spoken.

Can you do your duty,
and wear your beauty
when wisdom arrives
like a rock through the window?

The Ribbon

Drowning in an ocean of questions

he wrote poetry 'till
the ribbon broke,
chewing on verses
that spat on his tongue;

he went skydiving
through windmills,
unscathed

this: the poetry of revolution,
the revolution of poetry
written, fought out
in the streets;

still, no excuses—
he put his fist through
the door of indifference.

Make of it
what you want,
but you will be found

wanting.

Reflection

re-flec-tion (ri flek'shan) n.

- the process of light, heat, or sound being reflected.
- an image formed by reflection.
- a sign.
- a source of shame or blame
- serious thought.

Crying Eyes

crying eyes
surround me
crying eyes
confound me

why these crying eyes?

why these drops
                    of tears
why these passing
                    years
that bring so much
                    change?

my crying eyes
betray me
as on bended knee
I pray me

to figments of imagination.

why these crying eyes?
why such surprise?

to all the beautifuls
that meet their end:
is beauty true forever?
is living dying never?

why these crying eyes
every time I
think of us?
what will be will
if it must.

whose testament
do I trust?

legends, fables, old
prophets, stories told.

old, old forevers
in our tears
and our

crying eyes.

A Roadside Marker

A roadside marker 'long the way:
remembrance of a bitter day.

A day of sadness and heartfelt loss;
to one side the cross has been tossed.

It lies now in the dirt and dust,
just as all surely must,

to fade each day to weathered grain,
piled upon by snow and rain.

Yet no matter how desperate may be the plight
to sunset's kiss we greet each night.

Standing On The Plains

Standing on the plains,
traveller, you know me.

You know cold
and desperate hunger.
You greet loneliness
as a friend.

Your family echoes
a thousand miles behind,
but your ears
are tuned for majesties
you may never find.

Ah, traveller, their arrows
can never target your mind,
too ephemeral is it for material monsters.

So, traveller, you see my fogs
as more than mere madness
or halcyon hallucinations.

For a few microseconds
we can celebrate our knowledge,
then move on.

There are other encounters.

Free Rein

it should be given
free rein

it should be given
light

and no place
to hide

it should try its luck,
take a chance

see if there is music
and dance

so rouse it,
drag it from its berth

find the treasure
there to unearth—

for how long
can this fortune smile?

for how long
can we assume

we may shine away
the dust and gloom?

Chords

Chords, over and over again,
chords from I can't
remember when.

It's like that sometimes,
when reason cries
for the seasons' passing.

I Suppose

I suppose it's between

the two

hidden between
a dream or two.

I suppose

up /down
happy/sad
good/bad

it's somewhere between

the two.

That pinpoint
in the oceans

of time—
that fine
dividing line

so concise
so precise

the perfection of
a beautiful balance,
the harmonies of
happen-stance.

Balance, yes, balance—
that's the thing.

That elusive
hidden place
with all the demons
we must meet
face to face.

I'll stare them
down
to where they make
no sound,

keep them quiet
inside my head.

I'll muffle, and stifle
all the clamour—
no more sin
to enamour!

I suppose it's between
the two . . .
good/evil

that's where we land
with 'chutes
deployed,
both feet
on the ground:
landing quiet,
making

no sound,
either within
or
without.

Right on
that pinpoint

in the oceans

of time.

This Body

this body that
my soul wears
like an overcoat,
tattered and torn,
but my warm favourite,
it will be discarded, eventually.

What is left
will be the best part of me.

Acceptance

ac-cept (ak sept`) v.

1. agree to receive or do something offered
2. believe to be valid or correct
3. admit responsibility for something
4. make someone welcome
5. put up with something unwelcome.

derivative **acceptance n.**

Acceptance

Sometimes there is no why;
nothing to explain,
nothing to make plain,
no hope to hold,
no story to be told . . .

Sometimes there is
just what we see;
nothing of how it came to be.

Sometimes there is no why,
sometimes we can
only cry.

Bijou's Anthem[3]

Praise to her love,
It beckons through my desperation.
Praise to her love,
I was her one adoration.
Wonders galore,
How could I have asked for more?
She was the sum of creation.

Praise to her love,
It is my pure inspiration.
Praise to her love,
It is my true consolation.
As each day dawned,
What cloak of beauty was on?
Miracles without cessation.

Praise to her love,
It thrilled me beyond recognition.
Praise to her love,
It lifts me beyond exaltation.
The love in her voice
Left me without any choice
But to join her celebration.

3 Acknowledgement to Charles Wesley's "Praise to The Lord"

Praise to her love,
I sit in rapt contemplation.
Praise to her love,
She gave without hesitation.
Her miracles all
Before which I humbly fall,
My soul in total occupation.

And at my end
The ache in my heart will mend
And I will know
Love's Salvation.

Sailing

Sailing,
we will be sailing
through the clouds
through the dream
that we lived.

Our story told
in love
to behold.

Sailing,
we will be sailing
in the together,
the We
of You and Me—
how we were meant to be
before the time of seas.

Before any form or substance,
no previews or sequels
to be seen,
life only as a dream.

Visions,
yes, visions
were foretold:

How you would
die young,
never to be old.

Too much youth
too much vigour
too much beauty
to spoil,
so in my tears
I toil
to meet the requiem
of our fate.

Sailing,
we will be sailing,
our tears banished,
our hunger
for each other
vanished.

Some day together again
when that day will never end.

Sailing through clouds,
sailing on the breeze
sailing on our love
at our ease.

Leaving death behind,
no memory of any kind —
only our love,
our love light,
our sailing so bright
our sailing delight.

How any came to be:
came to be me
came to be you
came to be one
one out of two
two into one,
forged to be real,
two into one
forged,
then sealed.

Sealed beyond death's kiss—
sealed to see us as we're
sailing through bliss.

The bliss
that we lived,
the bliss
that we kissed,
taking bliss into life with
no sorrow or strife.

How two became one
then became three,
the pursuit of
love's mystery.
The why and the where
and the how,
when lords and kings
and precious things
take their bow,
when we took our vow
to have and to hold
to never be old
with futures untold.

Is there more mystery
to unravel,
more star roads
to travel?

With who, then?
With you, then?

You, not here,
but near.
So near
I can feel you.

How do I grasp the air?
How do I caress a memory?
How do I listen to silence?

What of these
enigmatic signals?
Do I read
the tea leaves
of love?
Do I stand down?
Give up the chase?
Wait to be taken?
or
just go sailing?

You must know by now
my deepest, most abiding vow
is to you.
That my love for you
is pure and true, and
that I will never
leave you.

So put away
that faraway stare.
Wrap your arms
around me.

I will lift you
to the stars,
hold your heart
to my breast.

Live the life
of
eternal rest.

The sweetest of all loves:
we will be
sailing.

My Starburst Girl

Starburst Girl
outshines that summer sun!
First time I saw
those starburst eyes
those starlight eyes
those star-joy eyes,
your spirit so strong:
you were a lioness, truly.

Bouncy and boundless
with dancing bright eyes
wide in wonder.

Radiant star-sparkle eyes
bewitched me.
None more fetching—
glorious energy of innocence!
Yet so worldly.

A natural, loving girl—
but a woman, too.

Worldly love,
Innocent love.

All chipmunks are Alvin,
bird rescuer supreme,
blue jay, why screech at mom?

Yes, earth mother, Starburst Girl,
lioness of love,
caring, with child-like voice,
of nature bonded.

Little-girl voice—
wide-eyed wonder—
new life you bring
into this world!

Starburst Girl,
a mother now:
daughter will follow.

Fierce devotion,
like sisters
caring for each other,
together.
Special
for always.

Starburst Girl,
star-sparkle girl,
and another to follow.
I, amazed, pleased,
honoured, humbled.

My Starburst Girl,
never braver—
none braver—
none stronger—
none more loving
than she.

Supernova lover,
fierce lioness of pride.

My girl,
you never age;
just wear different
shades of beautiful.

Impish prankster,
decorator,
baker,
giving her love
with food.

Radiant girl,
Bright girl,
Happy girl,
now tired girl ,
now breathless girl.

Eyes gone.
Memory, now
stronger than death,
bolts me time and again.

Spirit now
waiting true:
me stuck behind,
casting lines of sorrow
to the heavens
where you lay.

Oh! Starburst Girl,
warm me still,
radiate me still
with your love,
your undying love.
My forever Starburst Girl.

Let me weep for you
some more—
Each tear payment
for our love!

Each drop nourishes
like soft, warm rain
on the fertile soil
of our life long loving.

Let my tears
drive away your pain.
Let my tears
wash away the beast
that pervaded your body
but never touched
your loving spirit.

Let that calm
that comes after my weeping
tell you how blessed
I have been
to share your life,
and yes, your death
with you.

As I cherished you in life,
I now caress your loving memory.

Memory so profound
of what we meant
to each other.

My pain means
the beast can never again
touch you, never hurt you,
never more defile your happy nature.

Remembering always
this elegant girl: your
precious, refined beauty.

And so spirited.
Wore everything well.
Made it better.
Made me better.

Saved my soul with your love.

Your pure, natural love
that words are
too meager to describe,
and which I am so eager
to embrace again.

Peace for your Spirit,
Starburst Girl.

My only hope,
our only Salvation, is
Starburst Love forever.

August 16 , 2017

In my every breath
I hear her voice,
Her laughter and her love
painting the landscape
of my soul.

All the beautiful things
begin and end
with Diane.

CPSIA information can be obtained
at www.ICGtesting.com
Printed in the USA
LVOW06s1402261217
560762LV00005B/5/P

9 781525 514593